What Happens When We Recycle

Plastic?

Jillian Powell

W

FRANKLIN WATTS
LONDON·SYDNEY

This edition copyright © Franklin Watts 2014

Franklin Watts
338 Euston Road
London NW1 3BH

Franklin Watts Australia
Level 17/207 Kent Street
Sydney NSW 2000

Editor: Julia Bird
Designer: DR Ink
Art Director: Jonathan Hair

Picture credits: Ulrich Baumgarten/vario images/Alamy: 13b;
John Cancalosi/Nature PL: 10; Martyn Chillmaid/Science Photo
Library; 6; Construction Photography/Corbis: front cover bl;
Stephen Dorey/Alamy: 25b; Bob Edwards/Science Photo Library:
18; Graham Flack/Waste Watch: 9; Andrew Fox/Corbis: 12;
John A Giordano/Corbis: 14b; Angela Hampton/Ecoscene: 23;
James Holmes/Zedcor/Science Photo Library: 20, 21; James
King-Holmes/Science Photo Library: 16t; Image 100/Corbis: 8b;
Andrew Kendall/Shutterstock: front cover br; Grantly
Lynch/Alamy: 8t; Richard Nowitz/Corbis: 19.
Kate Peters/Ecoscene: 24; Ray Roberts/Ecoscene: 22.
Schegelmilch/Corbis: 7; TNT Magazine/Alamy: 13t.
Alan Towse/Ecoscene/Corbis: 15t, 16b, 17; Andrew
Twort/Alamy: 25t; Waste Watch: 14t.
Wonderlandstock?Alamy: front cover t, 11.

A CIP catalogue record for this book
is available from the British Library

ISBN: 978 1 4451 3031 6

Dewey Classification: 363.72'88

Printed in China

Franklin Watts is a division of
Hachette Children's Books,
an Hachette UK company.
www.hachette.co.uk

604.6

Contents

About plastics

● Useful plastics

Plastics were **invented** about 150 years ago. Most are made from oil, gas or coal. We now use plastics to make everything from bottles to toys, credit cards, computers, mobile phones, window frames and doors.

Many everyday things are made from plastic.

● Different types

There are thousands of different types of plastic. They are strong, light **materials**, which can be hard or soft, bendy or stiff, smooth or sticky. The type of plastic depends on the **polymers** from which it is made.

?

DID YOU KNOW?

Polymers are made from long chains of tiny **molecules**. Wool and wax are natural polymers. Plastics are man-made polymers.

Special uses

Some plastics can keep food and drinks fresh, protect them from light and keep them hot or cold, dry or moist. Other plastics are used to make electronic goods, as well as racing car and aircraft parts.

Racing cars are made of tough, light plastic and metal.

Some types of plastic	Uses
Polyethylene	(PET) water and fizzy drink bottles (HDPE) milk and **detergent** bottles
Polystyrene	egg cartons, cups, takeaway boxes
Acrylics	fibre fill duvets, jackets
PVC	food trays, cling film
Polypropylene	yogurt pots, margarine tubs, shampoo bottles

How we use plastics

● Important material

Plastics are a very important building and packaging material. Worldwide, we use around 100 million tonnes of plastic every year. In the UK alone we use around 5 million tonnes of plastic each year.

We use 17.5 billion plastic bags in the UK every year - that's about 290 bags per person!

Supermarkets pack many food products in plastic trays and wraps.

● Plastic packaging

Nearly half of all the packaging we use is made from plastic. It is used to hold or wrap food and drinks, household cleaners, batteries, gadgets and machines. Most plastic packaging is only used for a short time before it is thrown away.

Plastic waste

Plastics make up about 11% of our household rubbish, almost half of which is plastic bottles. Some plastics are **recycled** or burned to make **energy**. The rest are dumped in **landfill sites**.

JUST THE FACTS

• We recycle about 20% of our plastic bottles, and just 7% of our total plastic waste.

• The average household in the UK uses around 500 plastic bottles a year and recycles about 130.

About 80% of plastic bottles in the UK end up in landfill sites.

Why recycle plastics?

Plastic litter

When plastics are dumped on landfill sites, they stay there for hundreds of years because they don't rot away. Plastic litter can also harm wildlife if they eat or get caught up in it.

Reducing waste

Recycling plastic reduces the amount of plastic thrown away. It also saves on the **raw materials** used to make new plastics. Making plastics uses 8% of the world's oil as well as natural gas or coal, land and water. Oil, gas and coal are **non-renewable** fuels which means that one day, they will run out.

Bags and other plastic litter kill around a million sea creatures every year.

Saving energy

Making new plastics also uses energy and creates **carbon gases** that are contributing to **climate change**. Recycling plastics, rather than making them from new, can cut the energy used by two thirds and reduces waste gases by a third.

Recycling your plastic bottles helps the planet in lots of ways!

Collection

● Recycling boxes

Some plastic is collected from households in recycling boxes. Recycling vans collect the boxes and separate the different types of rubbish such as plastics, glass jars and paper.

● Recycling bins

You can also take some plastics to recycling bins. Some bins are just for plastics. Others are auto-sort machines that collect mixed rubbish. They use cameras, **infra-red** light and air jets to **sort** different materials.

All recyclable plastics can be put into a recycling bin.

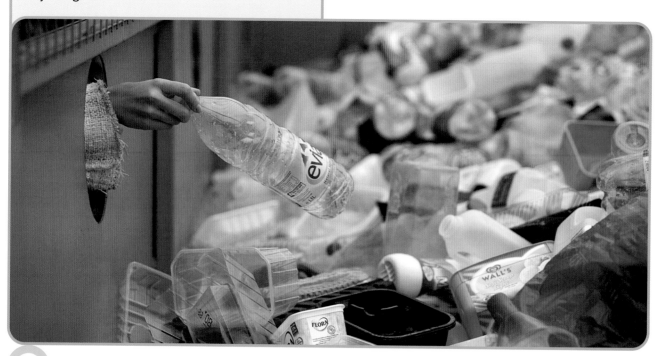

Recycling triangle

Some types of plastic are easier to recycle than others. Most plastics have a mark that shows the type of polymers they are made from. It is a triangle with letters such as PET or PVC.

PET bottles are 100% recyclable, but the caps are usually made from a different sort of plastic so they should be removed.

Each bale can contain thousands of plastic bottles.

Plastic bales

Lorries collect the plastics and deliver them to sorting centres where they are squashed and packed into bales, ready for the recycling plant.

GREEN GUIDE

You can help by rinsing and squashing plastic bottles before recycling. Most recycling bins and boxes take water and milk or detergent bottles, but can't recycle plastics such as yogurt pots or margarine tubs. Check your local council website for details.

Sorting

● Breaking up

The bales are taken to plastic recycling plants. Machines break up the bales, then the plastics are sent into the recycling plant on **conveyor belts**.

● Hand sorting

Before they can be recycled, plastics have to be sorted by colour and polymer type. At some plants, workers sort plastics by hand as they move past on a conveyor belt.

Workers wear thick gloves to protect their hands.

Conveyor belts carry plastics to the x-ray sorting machine.

?

DID YOU KNOW?

Infra-red can tell different plastics by the way the light rays **reflect** off them. Each type of plastic has its own infra-red 'signature'.

● Machine sorting

Some recycling plants have machines to sort plastics. They use x-rays or infra-red light to sort the different types. As the light rays bounce off the plastic, they send a signal to a computer that can tell the colour and type of plastic. The machines then use air jets to separate out the different plastics.

Shredding and cleaning

Shredding

After the plastics have been sorted, huge cutting wheels shred the plastics into small pieces. These are called plastic 'flakes'.

Plastic flakes come in many different colours.

This recycling plant is using a flotation tank to clean the plastic flakes.

Flotation tank

The flakes go through several stages of washing. Some plants use **flotation tanks** to separate the flakes from plastic caps and other bits of waste. In the tanks, the plastic flakes float and rise to the top, and heavier bits sink to the bottom.

DID YOU KNOW? **?**

When an object's weight is less than the weight of the water it **displaces**, it floats. When its weight is heavier, it sinks.

Cleaning

The flakes go into a washing machine that cleans out any bits of leftover food or drink waste. It also removes other waste materials like labels, foil or glue.

These freshly washed and dried flakes are now ready to be recycled.

Drying

When they have been washed clean, the plastic flakes go into a machine that spins them dry.

Melting

Heating

The clean plastic flakes are fed into a machine that heats them until they begin to melt. **Molten** plastic is soft and sticky.

DID YOU KNOW? **?**

Different types of plastics melt at different temperatures.

Screening

The molten plastic is then pushed or **extruded** through a metal plate which has tiny holes in it. The molten plastic comes out the other side in long strands, a bit like spaghetti.

This machine turns the melted plastic into long strands.

Pellets

The strands are cooled in water. Then they pass through a machine that chops them into small pieces all the same size. These are called plastic **pellets** or **granules**.

These plastic pellets will be melted and shaped to make new products.

New plastic

The pellets are sent along moving conveyor belts into big storage drums. From here, they are packed and sent to factories to be made into new plastic products.

Moulding

Plastic pellets

When the plastic pellets are heated, they melt. The molten plastic can have colours added and be shaped and stretched into different forms.

Colours can be added to the molten plastic.

This machine is winding polythene sheets made from recycled pellets.

Methods

Plastic can be **moulded** in many ways. It can be heated and squeezed into **moulds** to make cups or toys. Molten plastic can also be squeezed through holes to make sheets, tubes or pipes. It can have air blown inside it to make bottles or drums. It can also be sprayed through tiny holes in a strainer to make plastic **fibres**.

JUST THE FACTS

Many products, from bottles and toothbrushes to garden furniture, are made from 100% recycled plastics. Others are made from recycled pellets mixed with new plastic. Some products have a mark showing the recycled content.

New products

Range of goods

Recycled plastics can be used to make many things, from CD cases to bags, garden furniture, fences, window frames and doors.

These ropes are made from recycled plastic bags.

Types of plastic

Different plastics are recycled for different purposes.

- PVC plastics can be recycled as plastic tiles, flooring and pipes for drains and plumbing.

- HDPE plastic can be recycled as detergent bottles, crates, compost and waste bins and plastic furniture.

> 25 two-litre PET bottles will make a fleece.

- PET bottles can be recycled as water or detergent bottles, or as many other products, including carpets and even fleece jackets!

- Recycled plastic fibres can be used to fill ski jackets, sleeping bags and duvets.

- Plastic board and foam can be used to **insulate** homes and cut energy waste.

GREEN GUIDE

Plastic bubblewrap is a good insulating material. The tiny pockets trap air which helps to keep warmth in.

JUST THE FACTS

- 40 PET bottles make 1 square metre of carpeting.
- Insulating a house can reduce energy waste by up to 30%.

Degradable plastics

Some plastics are now **degradable** which means they rot away in time. These include plastics which break down in sunlight. But these **bio-plastics** release carbon gases when they rot in landfill sites and can't be recycled with other plastics.

Re-using and reducing

● Re-use

We can all help to reduce waste by re-using plastics. We can wash and re-fill plastic bottles or boxes. We can also re-use them for art or craftwork or to grow or cover plant seeds.

● Reduce

We can also easily reduce the amount of plastic we use. Taking your own bags when you go shopping is easy to do and makes a real difference.

GREEN GUIDE

Squeezy bottles can be washed out and used to water seeds.

These seedlings are being grown in an old plastic food container.

These chicks are made from recycled plastic bags.

Arts and crafts

Some artists recycle plastics by using them to make prints, collages or sculptures.

These boys have made a football out of old plastic bags.

New uses

In **developing countries**, people often have less money to spend on new things, so they make the most of what they have. Old plastic objects are turned into new and surprising things, such as colourful **woven** handbags or toys and games.

What you can do

At Stratherrick Primary School in Scotland, pupils collected plastic bottles to make into a greenhouse for the school wildlife garden. They spent six months collecting two-litre plastic bottles and three days building the greenhouse from around 1500 bottles. The pupils will use it to grow tomatoes and other fruits for the school kitchen and to take home. The project won first prize in a competition for environmental projects awarded by BBC Radio Scotland.

5 top tips for plastic recyclers:

1 Try to buy things made from recyclable plastics.

2 Remove bottle tops and lids before recycling.

3 Wash and squash plastics.

4 Re-use plastic bags.

5 Wash and re-use tubs or bottles.

Seed-propagator

You will need:

Plastic yogurt pots

Green craft paint and brush

Two clear plastic tubs (these should fit together; the top one deeper than the bottom one)

Seed compost

Seeds

Scissors

Step 1
Wash and dry the yogurt pots, then paint the outside of the pots green and allow to dry.

Step 2
Use the scissors to make three small holes in the bottom of each pot for drainage.

Step 3
Fill each pot with compost, leaving around one centimetre at the top.

Step 4
Plant the seeds following the instructions on the packet, then water well.

Step 5
Place the pots into the shallow tub and place the deeper tub over the top to make the mini-propagator. Place on a windowsill and keep the seeds watered. Watch the seeds grow!

Glossary

Bio-plastics Plastics made from corn or other plant sugars.

Carbon gases Gases from cars and industry that are believed to cause climate change.

Climate change A gradual change in the world's climate, caused by gases from cars and industry.

Conveyor belts Moving belts which transport things, for example through a recycling plant or factory.

Degradable Able to rot away

Developing countries Countries where industry is still developing and most people still farm the land to earn a living.

Detergent A substance used for washing or cleaning.

Displaces Takes the place of; replaces.

Energy Power or heat.

Extruded To shape plastic by pushing it through a metal plate with holes in it.

Fibres Tiny thread-like pieces

Flotation tanks Big tanks filled with water that cause some materials to float.

Granules Grains or pieces.

Infra-red A kind of light ray.

Insulate To line something with material that keeps warmth in.

Invented When something new is created.

Landfill sites Places where rubbish is buried under the ground.

Materials Substances that something else is made from.

Molecules The smallest bits or parts of a substance.

Molten When something solid melts and becomes liquid.

Moulds Containers that shape materials as they harden.

Moulded Shaped or formed.

Non-renewable Something that will run out one day: the sun, waves and wind provide renewable energy; coal, gas and oil are non-renewable sources of energy.

Pellets Small pieces.

Polymers Natural or manmade materials made from chains of molecules.

Raw materials Natural materials, such as wood and water.

Recycled When something, such as a material, is used again.

Reflect Bounce back.

Sort To arrange by type.

Woven Made by weaving strands of material together.

X-rays Electro-magnetic rays that can pass through solid materials.

Further information

Books

A Plastic Bottle's Journey (Follow It!) Suzanne Slade, Picture Window Books 2011

Plastic – Reduce, Reuse, Recycle Alexandra Fix, Heinemann 2007

Plastic – Reusing and Recycling Ruth Thomson, Franklin Watts 2009

Websites

www.petcore-europe.org

Website that focuses on recycling PET plastics.

www.recoup.org

Fact sheets, links and information from a charity set up to develop plastics recycling.

www.recyclenow.com

Lots of information on all kinds of recycling, with a section on plastics.

Note to parents and teachers: Every effort has been made by the Publishers to ensure that the websites in this book are suitable for children, that they are of the highest educational value, and that they contain no inappropriate or offensive material. However, because of the nature of the Internet, it is impossible to guarantee that the contents of these sites will not be altered. We strongly advise that Internet access is supervised by a responsible adult.

Index